HOW TO BOUNCE BACK FROM WHATEVER LIFE THROWS YOUR WAY!

MASTERING RESILIENCE & DETERMINATION

Table of Contents

What does life throw your way? 1

If things will always happen, what can i do to change the situation? . 2

Why a course on "bouncing back"? 3

What about trauma, tragedy, big loss, illness or even death 4

My story..5

What you will learn in this course...6

Meet mitch 7

My own massive transformation 8

Meet mitch 9

What is resilience? 10

What did this study show?..11

Is failure a stepping stone to success? 12

Check out these stories:oichiro honda 13

J.K. Rowling 14

Martha stewart 15

Ratan tata 16

6. Steve jobs...17

Walt disney...18

Henry ford...19

Thomas edison 20

Two real life stories of adversity 21

10 Strategies resilient people use to bounce back when life knocks them down...22

Resilience is a life story...23

1. Laughter positivity and hope 24

2. Accepting and anticipating change on a...25

3. Embracing the power of choice 26

4. Asking for help 27

5. Being self aware and connected..28

6. Living to learn 29

7. Valuing the importance of health & well-being 30

9. Embrace failure and disappointment..31

10. Be adaptable, flexible and flow 32

Other strategies i use 33

Tools for your toolkit:acceptance 34

Flexibility...35

Get perspective-know when to ask for help 36

Let it go 37

Have an attitude of gratitude...38

Stress management 39

Best tool ever 40

Great resources on bouncing back & resiliency 41

Key take-aways from this course..42

Next steps on your healing journey...43

- Disappointment, betrayal, loss, abuse, overwhelm, sadness, disease, death, inability to cope with life on your terms, or just total mayhem?

- Life is a fairly complex machine with many moving parts

- Stuff is always happening (sometimes triage), but one thing is for certain...

- The more things change...the more they stay the same (at least according to the law of physics)

- But, when the sh-t hits the fan, it seems like we'll never recover from the trauma and shock

- There's a lot we can do about things that happen to us, for us, or because of us

- 3 things exactly: we can do nothing, do something or accept it

- By doing nothing or ignoring it, the problem never really goes away, but it doesn't seem as bad. Will it rear it's ugly head once again or even get worse? Maybe

- It's like putting some adhesive tape or a bandaid on a leak with your kitchen sink pipe. The root problem still exists, but the it's sure not leaking as much water.

- Because it is necessary if you don't want to be defeated, stay stuck, and move on with you life

- Staying stuck or bouncing back is a choice that requires courage, determination, self-will, and determination

- We must understand and learn from what set us back so that we don't repeat the mistakes or temporary setbacks

- It is a process that if mastered, can help you navigate and succeed beautifully in life

- What we learn from bouncing back from anything will help us grow and prosper in life

- Sometimes bad things happen to good people

- Often it's nobody's fault, but we're never prepared for the big stuff

- Like grieving the death of a loved one or your house burning down, there is a grieving and mourning process we must go through, or insurance company to call to rebuild.

- But, what if you lost your job that you loved or needed, or one of your kids was hooked on drugs, or perhaps you were abused as a young child, or maybe you lost all your life savings because of a crooked stockbroker, or worse, you found yourself in jail, divorced, and on the street without any resources or a clear mind.

- What would you do?

MY STORY...

- My story is all about overcoming adversity and learning to bounce back no matter what

- I've had 12 businesses, 3 of which were very successful, some of which failed. But, I NEVER gave up trying. I learned something new and important each time

- I lost everything in my life at middle-age, and nearly died twice from addiction. I was homeless, penniless, and destitute. I had lost all hope and wanted to die. Suicide & misery were not an option for me, and I chose life

- My crawl back to a good life took time, determination, lots of disappointment along the way, but my desire to succeed was strong and I can now overcome anything that comes my way – and it will!

- I learned some incredibly invaluable lessons that I will share with you. My biggest strength is my resilience and determination. I have always had the prize in sight and never gave up!

- You can do this too, and while it may seem dark at times, there is tremendous reward, growth and satisfaction in the light at the other end of the tunnel. So, let's do this!!

- How we can prepare ourselves and learn the skills to bounce back from anything that happens to you – no matter how big, shocking, or bad

- How learning to be resilient will change your life even if nothing happens

- How to eliminate and manage the roadblocks that get in your way of reaching your goals and dreams

- How to not be a victim or do the blame game to others

- How to take responsibility for anything and everything that happens in your life

MEET MITCH

21-DAY HAPPINESS
WORKOUT & KICKSTART
M. Fenton Deutsch
REVOLUTIONARY, NEW WAY
TO BEAT THE BLUES
& TRANSFORM YOUR LIFE
HAPPINESS
HEROES
FREEDOM
REVOLUTION

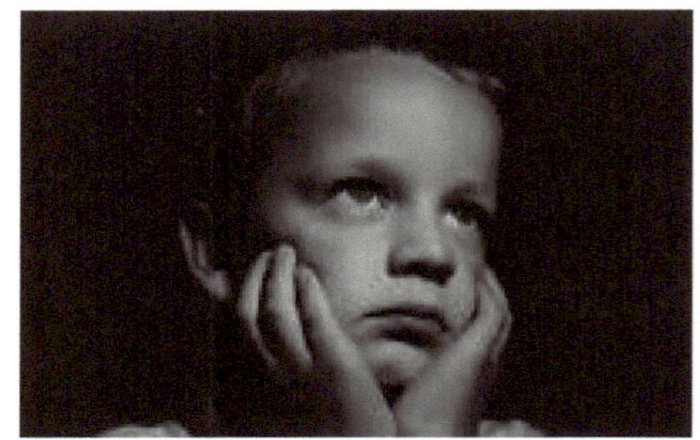

Mitch Before @ Age 55

Mitch After @ Age 62

- 310 lbs.
- *On 15 Medications
- Walking with a cane
- Workaholic
- Addicted to Alcohol & Pills
- Kids & ex-wife hate me
- Few Friends
- Angry & Burnt Out
- Lonely, Irritable, Discontent
- Couch Potato
- Very Sad & Mad

- 199 lbs.
- *Medication Free
- *Workout 5 days/week – totally buff
- Doing what I love with total balance
- Substance Free
- Healed relationships with Family & Friends
- Deep & Loving Friendships at home and at work.
- Free from my past and living in the incredible flow and gifts of my life.
- Meditate & do Yoga, Spin & Cross Fit
- Happy, fulfilled & smiling, relaxed & truly grateful to be alive! At peace with my life & the universe

21-DAY HAPPINESS
WORKOUT & KICKSTART
M. Fenton Deutsch
REVOLUTIONARY, NEW WAY
TO BEAT THE BLUES
& TRANSFORM YOUR LIFE
HAPPINESS
HEROES
FREEDOM
REVOLUTION

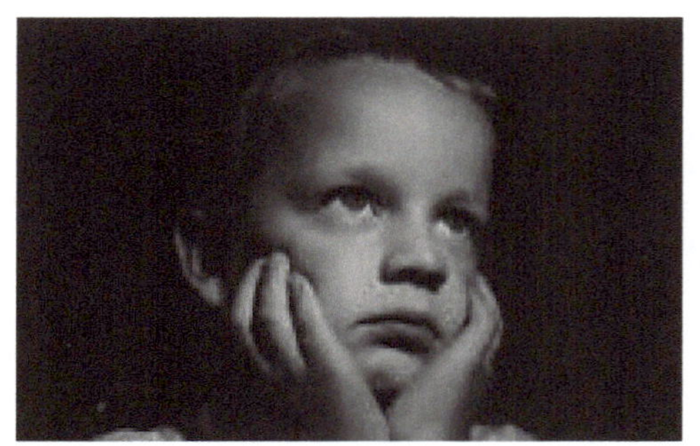

- According to the New York Times, (Bouncing Back From Hard Times by Tony Bilanow) "resilience is the ability to rebound from hardships like a serious health problem, the death of a family member, debt or other ills.

- "New research suggests that resilience may have at least as much to do with how often people have faced adversity in the past as it does with who they are — their personality, their genes, for example — or what they're facing now. That is, the number of life blows a person has taken may affect his or her mental toughness more than any other factor," he writes.

- Source: New York Times, Read the full article here, "On Road to Recovery, Past Adversity Provides a Map."

- "Interestingly, in one recent study that monitored the mental well-being of nearly 2,000 adults for several years, it wasn't those who had never suffered a major setback, or those who had suffered the most, who fared best:

- It was those in the middle, those reporting two to six stressful events, who scored highest on several measures of well-being, and who showed the most resilience in response to recent hits.

- In short, the findings suggest that mental toughness is something like physical strength: It cannot develop without exercise, and it breaks down when overworked. Some people in the study reported having had more than a dozen stressful events, and it showed."

- Source: New York Times, Read the full article here, "On Road to Recovery, Past Adversity Provides a Map."

- It is said that failure is the stepping stone to success. But what if failure, like a cursed omen, keeps repeating itself in one's life and brings them disappointment and depression? At such times, patience, perseverance and characters are tested. It is during this time that human nature bounces back and proves its mettle. No matter how bad the situation, when the going gets tough, the tough get going.

- "Imagine your entire factory being bombed twice, and then crumbling a third time after an earthquake! If we were Soichiro Honda, we would have thought that it's destiny that doesn't want us to build a business. However, Soichiro had no such thoughts. The founder of Honda automobiles did not give up despite his factory being bombed twice in World War ll. He then thought of making a bicycle that had a small motor in it. The scooter was then exported to the US and it was a huge hit. Thereon began the successful journey of an entrepreneur who never looked back."

- Before getting her Potter books published, J.K. Rowling used to consider herself a failure. She was jobless, divorced and penniless. She had a kid, whom she couldn't take good care of due to having no money. It was after her divorce that she started writing Harry Potter. In 1995, around 12 major publishing houses rejected Harry Potter. Two years later, Bloomsbury decided to take it up and the rest is history.

- Back in this century, Stewart, the founder of the company that bears her name, was America's first self-made female billionaire. Five years after her company went public, however, Stewart went to prison for conspiracy as part of the ImClone stock case.

- And then she went gently into that good night…. Heck no, she didn't! Stewart launched her comeback campaign immediately after her release. Her company was profitable again within a year, and she rejoined its board of directors in 2011. She currently serves as chairman.

- When Tata Indica was showing no signs of progress, Ratan Tata decided to approach Ford to sell the car project. The Tatas went to Detroit, where they met Bill Ford who taunted Ratan Tata by saying, "Why did you enter in the passenger car business when you were not knowing of it? It will be favor if we buy this business from you". This made Tata withdraw the offer. A couple of years later, when Ford was in losses, Tata group was offered the deal of buying Jaguar-Land Rover. At that time, Bill Ford said to Ratan Tata, "You are doing a big favour for us by buying Jaguar- Land Rover". Now that's a comebac

- Let's not forget that the co-founder of Apple was fired from his own company! Steve Jobs rose like a phoenix after he was ousted from Apple. He then focussed on Next and Pixar and then returned to Apple to take it over from where he left. In a commencement speech, Steve Jobs has mentioned that getting fired from Apple was the best thing that could have ever happened to him.

- The creator of Mickey Mouse tasted failure first when he went bankrupt after the failure of a cartoon series in Kansas City. Disney then headed to LA with $40 in cash, and an imitation-leather suitcase containing only a shirt, two undershorts, two pairs of socks and some drawing materials. He badly wanted to be an actor. However, life had some different plans for him. He and his brother then decided to open an animation studio in California. Look what that became!

- • Believe it or not, Henry Ford went bankrupt five times! But that didn't stop him from becoming the man who revolutionised industrial production. Ford was a farm boy who started as a machine shop apprentice. He then went on to become chief engineer. In 1893, he built his first car and from there on he struggled to bring down the cost of production, which eventually led to the production of affordable cars.

- The inventor failed 1,000 times while inventing the light bulb! He even gave the now famous quote - "I have not failed 10,000 times. I have not failed once. I have succeeded in proving that those 10,000 ways will not work. When I have eliminated the ways that will not work, I will find the way that will work." Now, that's how one should approach failure

- Source: Taken from 11 Inspiring Stories Of People Who Bounced Back After Failing https://www.indiatimes.com/culture/who-we-are/11-inspiring-stories-of-people-who-bounced-back-after-failing-269768.html

TWO REAL LIFE STORIES OF ADVERSITY

- Having survived my share of life's blows, starting as a child with an alcoholic parent and moving on to the usual bouts of unemployment, heartbreaks, etc., I know that for me there is nothing more empowering than knowing that I have been through tough times and lived to tell about it. I did it then, and I can do it again, if need be. Though I hope I won't have to. -- anonymous

- Adversity can make you stronger but it can also traumatize you to the point of being either scared to death or numb. 10 years ago my husband's job was downsized – during my eight month of pregnancy. We sold our furniture and few valuables and moved East. Over the course of the next two years we had our vehicles repossessed, had to live in a one bedroom basement apartment (that's all we could afford)and was snubbed by my family who lived nearby because we weren't "fitting into the community" (a small upper class college town). We very slowly crawled out of the hole we were in and both eventually found good employment, paid off our debts and now live well with both of our automobiles paid for and no credit card debt.It wasn't our first experience with adversity – I had struggled with drug and alcohol problems when I was in my early twenties and my husband is Native American and was born and raised in dire poverty. But this last go round with unemployment/bill collectors/repo men and the estrangement of my family has affected us deeply. We still jump when the phone rings and wonder about the number on the caller ID even though we have no outstanding bills, we tiptoe to the door and look out the peephole when someone knocks, a minor car repair still causes an initial feeling of overwhelming despair until we remind ourselves that we can afford it, the rift with my family has never been repaired – the feeling of abandonment when we really needed support (and not money – just being there for the three of us) is still exquisitely painful. I guess adversity does make some folks stronger and in some ways, I do feel a little better at coping. Or maybe that's just due to the fact that I feel numb a lot of the time. anonymous

10 STRATEGIES RESILIENT PEOPLE USE TO BOUNCE BACK WHEN LIFE KNOCKS THEM DOWN

- "People who soar are those who refuse to sit back, sigh and wish things would change. They neither complain of their lot nor passively dream of some distant ship coming in. Rather, they visualize in their minds that they are not quitters, they will not allow life's circumstances to push them down and hold them under" Charles Swindoll

- "Resilience enables you to live a life that is based on choice rather than being at the mercy of chance or habit. It also enables you to manage adversity and "bounce back" when life has shot you down.

- When you are living a resilient life, you are living a fulfilled life, where you know who you are and you know what is important to you. You have a plan as to where you are going and you know where you should be investing your time and energy.

- For you to lead a resilient life you have to overcome the pain, the adversity and the unpredictable challenges that life throws at you. It is not an easy journey, but then again, life was not meant to be easy.

- The good news is that resilience is a process of thoughts and actions that can be learned. Although we can not control the challenging events in our lives, resilience can give us the strength to control our responses to these events."

- Source: Lifehack by Kathryn Sandford Career Resilience Coach passionate about supporting others to grow and thrive in a complex world https://www.lifehack.org/articles/communication/10-strategies-resilient-people-use-bounce-back-when-life-knocks-them-down.html

- "Resilience is intangible, as you can't touch it, but you can see and feel it. Resilience is a person's life story and to truly understand and feel resilience at work, you need listen to resilient people's stories. While you are listening to their stories, you will hear them talk about how they used various strategies to overcome the adversity and challenges in their life.

- There are the 10 strategies that resilient people commonly use to manage adversity and to "bounce back" when life has knocked them down. By using these 10 strategies and listening to the stories of resilient individuals, you will be shown HOW you can live a resilient and fulfilled life." Source: Lifehack by Kathryn Sandford Career Resilience Coach passionate about supporting others to grow and thrive in a complex worldhttps://www.lifehack.org/articles/communication/10-strategies-resilient-people-use-bounce-back-when-life-knocks-them-down.html

1. LAUGHTER POSITIVITY AND HOPE

- I like nonsense, it wakes up the brain cells. Fantasy is a necessary ingredient in living, it's a way of looking at life through the wrong end of a telescope. Which is what I do, and that enables you to laugh at life's realities." Dr Seuss

- Resilient people live meaningful lives. They love to laugh and have a positive and hopeful attitude of life. Resilient people don't take themselves too seriously and they have a sense of humour about the challenges of life.

- For resilient people, happiness comes because they believe in who they are, they know what they are doing, and they love what they do.

- Resilient people are optimistic and believe in their own strength and ability to overcome any problems. In a crisis, a resilient person will be positive, open and willing to find the solution. They will not be dwelling on the problem but looking forward to the future solutions that should be considered.

- Laughter, positivity and hope are important strateges to use when you want to build resilience in your life. by Kathryn Sandford Career Resilience Coach passionate about supporting others to grow and thrive in a complex worldhttps://www.lifehack.org/articles/communication/10-strategies-resilient-people-use-bounce-back-when-life-knocks-them-down.html

2. ACCEPTING AND ANTICIPATING CHANGE ON A

- In todays world of constant change it is hard to hold on to who you are and manage the complexity and unpredictability of life. The one constant thing in our lives today is change.

- Resilience is a quality that enables you to survive and thrive in a world of constant change. Resilient people are always ready for the unpredictable events in their lives. To them change is part of the daily routine of life. It is expected, and in fact, those who are most resilient embrace the opportunities that change brings.

- byKathryn Sandford Career Resilience Coach passionate about supporting others to grow and thrive in a complex worldhttps://www.lifehack.org/articles/communication/10-strategies-resilient-people-use-bounce-back-when-life-knocks-them-down.html

3. EMBRACING THE POWER OF CHOICE

- Today I choose life. Every morning when I wake up I can choose joy, happiness, negativity, pain… To feel the freedom that comes from being able to continue to make mistakes and choices – today I choose to feel life, not to deny my humanity but embrace it." Kevyn Aucion

- Resilient people are comfortable with using the power of choice. They understand the value of the power of choice when dealing with tough decisions or confronting challenging situations. Using the power of choice empowers and strengthens their ability to take action and to make decisions.

- They know that they are not responsible for the challenging events in their lives. They also know they are in control of their responses to these events. By embracing the power of choice, resilient people are able to maintain perspective and manage the flow of emotions that they are dealing with in the present moment.

- Resilient people are not afraid to to acknowledge their negative feelings, emotions and fears. Instead, they choose not to let these negative fears and emotions take control and immobilize them.

- by Kathryn Sandford Career Resilience Coach passionate about supporting others to grow and thrive in a complex worldhttps://www.lifehack.org/articles/communication/10-strategies-resilient-people-use-bounce-back-when-life-knocks-them-down.html

- "Asking for help does not mean that we are weak or incompetent. It usually indicates an advanced level of honesty and intelligence." Anne Wilson Schaef

- They value the input of others, along with the wisdom and energy to overcome the adversity or solve the problems they are facing. Resilient people do not work or live in isolation. They enjoy belonging to a community and have a very collaborative approach when it comes to decision making and problem solving

- by Kathryn Sandford Career Resilience Coach passionate about supporting others to grow and thrive in a complex worldhttps://www.lifehack.org/articles/communication/10-strategies-resilient-people-use-bounce-back-when-life-knocks-them-down.html

5. BEING SELF AWARE AND CONNECTED

- Resilient people practice the concept of mindfulness. They pay attention to where they are in the present moment. They are connected to what is important to them in their lives – family and friends. They know who they are and what they stand for.

- They are self-aware and are able to monitor the thoughts that flow through them. This allows them to be able to tolerate ambiguity and hold opposing thoughts in their minds at the same time. Instead of reacting to their negative thoughts they will observe these thoughts and then let them pass through like a storm.

- Their values and their purpose in life are the foundations from which they lead their lives. Any decision they need to make or any problem they need to solve will be aligned to their beliefs and values. by Kathryn Sandford Career Resilience Coach passionate about supporting others to grow and thrive in a complex worldhttps://www.lifehack.org/articles/communication/10-strategies-resilient-people-use-bounce-back-when-life-knocks-them-down.html

6. LIVING TO LEARN

- "By three methods we may learn wisdom: First, by reflection, which is noblest; Second, by imitation, which is easiest; and third by experience, which is the bitterest." Confucius

- Resilient people learn to take charge of their thinking and emotions in order to become resilient. They know that to live a resilient life they must continuously develop and strengthen their skills and abilities to remain strong.

- They are survivors and when faced with adversity will ask themselves, "How can I survive this and what do I need to do to overcome this obstacle?" They know their strengths and their vulnerabilities and they are solution-focused thinkers.

- They will always look for ways in which they can source the best solution for the problem or challenges they need to overcome. Resilient people are inquisitive, curious and questioning – always seeking information or new knowledge that will help them to be a better and stronger person.

- They acquire new skills and knowledge through life experience, observation, reflection and from the wisdom of others. They believe in the journey of continuous self-improvement and see life challenges and adversity as an opportunity to learn.

- Resilient people also understand that to live a resilient life one has to experience life – the good, the bad and the ugly.

- by Kathryn Sandford Career Resilience Coach passionate about supporting others to grow and thrive in a complex worldhttps://www.lifehack.org/articles/communication/10-strategies-resilient-people-use-bounce-back-when-life-knocks-them-down.html

- "Intelligence comes into being when...the mind, the heart and the body are really harmonious" J Krishnamurti

- The energy source of resilience comes from the physical and mental strength of a person. A resilient person understands the importance of being physically, emotionally and mentally fit. They understand the importance of consistently following daily healthy habits that nurture and strength their health and well-being. Resilient people look after themselves and value the gift of having a healthy and emotionally strong body and mind.

- They value the positive energy they get by surrounding themselves with like-minded people. This positive energy builds and maintains their emotional, physical and mental well-being. Resilient people have healthy and strong relationships which they value and nurture.

- by Kathryn Sandford Career Resilience Coach passionate about supporting others to grow and thrive in a complex worldhttps://www.lifehack.org/articles/communication/10-strategies-resilient-people-use-bounce-back-when-life-knocks-them-down.html

9. EMBRACE FAILURE AND DISAPPOINTMENT

- "Character cannot be developed in ease and quiet. Only through experience of trial and suffering can the soul be strengthened, ambition inspired and success achieved" Helen Keller

- Resilient people have the mindset of a survivor and not a victim. They expect to make mistakes, to fail, and to be disappointed. They know that to be strong, one has to overcome adversity and failure.

- They embrace life learning experiences such as failure and disappointment because it enables them to grow and become a better person.

- Resilient people do not seek validation from others to determine their success. They define their success in their own terms.

- To help them define their key learnings and how they can move forward in their lives, resilient people will ask these three questions:

- 1. What went well?

- 2. What didn't go so well?

- 3. What can I do better next time?

- Those who are resilient do not typically have a fear of failure and they understand the importance of how they respond to their failures. Resilient people choose to respond to failure by "bouncing back" and starting again.

- by Kathryn Sandford Career Resilience Coach passionate about supporting others to grow and thrive in a complex worldhttps://www.lifehack.org/articles/communication/10-strategies-resilient-people-use-bounce-back-when-life-knocks-them-down.html

10. BE ADAPTABLE, FLEXIBLE AND FLOW

- "Be like water making its way through cracks. Do not be assertive, but adjust to the object, and you shall find a way 'round or through it. If nothing within you stays rigid, outward things will disclose themselves" Bruce Lee

- Resilient people understand that life is not static – it is unpredictable and challenging. Adaptability, flexibility and flow are key strengths that enable resilient people to manage the unpredictability of life. These three strengths are also essential for all the other nine resilient strategies that resilient people use to "bounce back" from the challenges of life.

- Adaptability, flexibility and flow give resilient people the capacity to cope internally with the complexity of life and the range of positive and negative emotions they will experience in their lives.

- If you want to live a resilient life, it is a tough journey because to be resilient you have to experience personal setbacks. This is undoubtedly scary, and for many of us, we choose not to embrace resilience and our life languishes. Resilient people know the huge effort and energy it takes to be able to "bounce back" from the challenges of life.

- They use these 10 strategies to build their strength and capacity to lead a resilient life. They choose to embrace the unpredictability of life, the pain and the adversity because they know that the rewards they gain from choosing a resilient life are priceless. It is easy to take these strategies and want to follow them to lead a resilient life, but to actually follow them and live by them is a feat all on its own. by Kathryn Sandford Career Resilience Coach passionate about supporting others to grow and thrive in a complex worldhttps://www.lifehack.org/articles/communication/10-strategies-resilient-people-use-bounce-back-when-life-knocks-them-down.html

OTHER STRATEGIES I USE

- It's not your fault, so stop feeling shame, guilt, or remorse which will keep you frozen in the past and immobilized.

- Stop blaming others (and yourself)

- Move on and mobilize – don't dwell on the small stuff, stay focused on the prize and go for it

- Move a Muscle, change a thought – one of my favorites – get out of your head and do something different

- Reframe: This is similar, but looking at your situation from another person's perspective, and ask what they would do

- Be positive in Life: look at the glass half-full and keep filling your tank

- Seek help through your own personal board of advisors, mentors, peers, loved ones – don't do adversity alone – there's lots of help (including lawyers, consultants and accoutants who go through this tough stuff everyday

- Get used to "The burn." it's most definitely temporary and will fade away shortly – be patient – as you're not the first person to overcome adversity

- Turn your adversity into gold. Every failure is a golden opportunity to turn a problem into a huge opportunity

- Never give uP. I never have and never will – why? I believe in myself and my abilities. What's more, I understand my mission in life

- If you can't change it, accept it

- Acceptance is usually the answer to most our problems today

- We learn the hard way that you can't put a square peg through a round hole

- After considering your options, sometimes accepting the situation as it is and not as you would have it is the best solution to dealing with adversity

- Some things like death, tragedy, total loss can't be changed, but how we deal with them can.

- We need to focus on getting better at how we process adversity and challenge

FLEXIBILITY

- Keep your options open and take a pause to consider your available options

- Sometimes taking no action is better than a rushed judgment or decision

- Stay calm, come to your senses, remove yourself from the situation, and then consider all the available options

- If one approach to solve the crisis doesn't work, it's not the end of the world (much like the crisis), but another opportunity to try another approach. Keep trying till you figure out the best solution

- Life is all about building perspective and making choices.

- When big stuff happens, you need to understand the problem and situation before making a difficult decision. Get the facts, take a deep breath, explore your options.

- Always get a second or many opinions. Knowledge is power – especially when you're in a pinch, and you'd be surprised what help comes your way WHEN you ask. It is my experience that people like to help and will be honored when you simply ask them.

- The faster we move out of the pain or our past and the fear of the future, the more we can stay focused on what's in front of us – the solution to the problem at hand is not the result of panic or fear. It may be a reaction to pain, but with some maturity and practice, you will approach it with a level head

- I use the serenity prayer to help make decisions: "Grant me the serenity to accept the things I cannot change, the courage to change the things I can, and the wisdom to know the difference."

- The wisdom comes from repetition, practice and experience – so know what you can't change, and take action to change the things you can right now!

HAVE AN ATTITUDE OF GRATITUDE

- A grateful person will never fail, because there is no such thing as failure – but just another glorious bump in the road to teach us something new about our life and the world.

- Being grateful is not something we're are naturally born with. Rather, it is practiced and gets better with time and appreciation.

- Keep a personal journal, and start a gratitude list. Your list doesn't have to be elaborate (the first time I wrote one, I couldn't think of anything except for my worn-out, red sneakers. That changed in time and I can write for pages today. You will soon come to appreciate, while bad things do happen, more good things happen than bad, and it's the good ones that we focus on and enhance who we are as human beings.

- Panic is often the "go-to" method that comes from the fear and the flight or fight response. It is important to move through this knee jerk reaction to trauma and stay cool. Here are some tips that work best:

- How to manage the stress from trauma and panic? Take care of yourself and your needs. Nothing gets done well and with a clear mind if you're hungry, lonely, angry, or tired (HALT). Avoid making rash decisions in the heat of the moment

- Get calm, meditate and transcend the pain and situation. No doubt you will choose the most appropriate solution

- Exercise as often as possible – especially in a crisis. You will calm down and feel better afterwards

- Don't anesthetize yourself with drugs or alcohol. You will never make a clear and wise decision when you can't think straight

- See a professional if you need counseling or have an immediate medical emergency. Don't be a stupid hero!

- "Everything happens for a reason, for our own good, and for the very best"– Ancient Jewish Mystical Wisdom – the Rebbe"

- "I have practiced and internalized this saying for years. It has become a way of life. My point? It is not important what happens to us, it is more important what we do about it. Further, I could not have possibly intuited or guessed how my life would turn out. I am grateful it did – G-d only knows it's been quite the ride – but it has taught me so much and made me so much smarter and stronger. If I did not experience all the pain I've encountered during my life, I would NOT be the person I am today. I have no regrets and wouldn't change a thing – even if I could. Really! This is my life, it is playing out the way it was intended, I have many choices and I've learned to choose wisely and with intent and perspective" – Mitch Deutsch

GREAT RESOURCES ON BOUNCING BACK & RESILIENCY

- https://www.ted.com/talks/raphael_rose_from_stress_to_resilience

- https://www.youtube.com/watch?v=HU3DsJ5aNZw

- https://www.youtube.com/watch?v=XePKBhrTxR0

- https://www.youtube.com/watch?v=X2UD4j9z13U

- https://ideas.ted.com/8-tips-to-help-you-become-more-resilient/

- https://www.inc.com/lolly-daskal/how-to-be-more-resilient-when-things-get-tough.html

- https://www.verywellmind.com/ways-to-become-more-resilient-2795063

- https://www.mindtools.com/pages/article/resilience.htm

- Best books: Failing Forward https://www.amazon.com/Failing-Forward-Turning-Mistakes-Stepping/dp/0785288570 https://www.youtube.com/watch?v=GqmTzy0FTr0

- Falling Upwards: https://www.amazon.com/Falling-Upward-Spirituality-Halves-Life/dp/0470907754 https://www.youtube.com/watch?v=4og_LyEsiN0

KEY TAKE-AWAYS FROM THIS COURSE

- Stuff happens – sometimes really bad stuff

- It is a fact of life – not good or bad – it just is

- Focus on the prize in life and stay focused no matter what happens

- Life is full of little and big bumps –they are inevitable and factual for all of us

- But, it's how we process the hardship and knocks in life that make us better, stronger

- Being a winner means knowing how to deal well with adversity

- Develop your inner strength, be grateful for whatever comes your way – because it will and give thanks that you are still breathing to see another day and try again.

- You will prevail if you choose to. You can do it and you must!!

- THE HEALING ACADEMY (url)/facebook group)

- Healing from Toxic Parents

- Happiness Mastery System

- 21-Day Happiness Challenge

- Making Love Work

- Making Life Work

- Spiritual Journey

- Mindfulness & Meditation

- All my e-books

www.ingramcontent.com/pod-product-compliance
Lightning Source LLC
Chambersburg PA
CBHW040049240726
48664CB00004B/1123